WORLD BOOK
looks at
AUSTRALIA

World Book, Inc.
a Scott Fetzer Company

Chicago   London   Sydney   Toronto

WORLD BOOK
looks at
AUSTRALIA

World Book looks at
Books in this series are based on information and illustrations contained in The World Book Encyclopedia.

Created and edited by Brian Williams and Brenda Williams
Designed by Tim Mayer

World Book, Inc.
525 W. Monroe
Chicago, Illinois 60661

For information on other World Book products, call 1-800-255-1750 x2238, or visit us at our Web site at http://www.worldbook.com

Library of Congress Cataloging-in-Publication Data
World book looks at Australia/ [created and edited by Brian Williams
    and Brenda Williams].
        p. cm.–(World book looks at)
        "...based on information and illustrations contained in the World
book encyclopedia"–Verso t.p.
    Includes index.
    Summary: Presents information about the geography, plant and
animal life, and culture of Australia.
    ISBN 0-7166-1814-1 (hc)   ISBN 0-7166-1815-x (sc)
    1. Australia–Juvenile literature. [1. Australia.]
I. Williams, Brian, 1943-   . II. Williams, Brenda. III. World
book encyclopedia. IV. Series.
DU96.W67 1998
994–dc21   97-22566

Printed in Singapore

1 2 3 4 5 6 7 8 9 10 99 98 97

CONTENTS

Introducing Australia

Australians know there is no other country in the world like Australia – and that's a fact!

Australia is the world's sixth largest country and the world's smallest continent. People often speak of Australia as "down under" because it lies entirely within the Southern Hemisphere.

Australia is a huge, dry land. Most of the country's 18 million people live near the coasts, where rainfall is highest. Most "Aussies" (as Australians are often called) are city dwellers, too.

Wide-open spaces

Australia is known for its vast open spaces, its bright sunshine, and its huge herds of sheep and cattle. It is also home to some of the world's most unusual animals, including kangaroos, koalas, wombats, and two "rule-breaking" mammals – the platypus and the echidna. They actually lay eggs!

So let's take a closer look "down under." Let's explore Australia.

Australia is surrounded by oceans, like an island (above). It is the only country that is also a continent. Australia is an ancient land with a vigorous present and a bright future. Exciting buildings like the famous Sydney Opera House (below), which opened in 1973, symbolize the nation's development as a leader in many fields.

The Flinders Ranges are towering mountains in South Australia. Wind and rain have eroded Australia's ancient rocks to form dramatic landscapes.

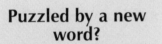

Puzzled by a new word?

To learn the meaning of a difficult or new word, turn to the glossary on page 62.

The echidna, or spiny anteater, is one of Australia's many unusual animals. Although it is a mammal, the echidna lays eggs.

The Big Country

Mount Kosciusko, Australia's highest point, is a snow-topped peak in the Australian Alps in New South Wales.

What kind of country is Australia? Let's take a look around. You'll be amazed by how big it is!

Highs and lows

Australia is mostly on the level. The highest mountains, sometimes called the Great Dividing Range, lie in the Eastern Highlands. The Australian Alps – part of the Eastern Highlands – include Australia's highest peak, Mount Kosciusko.

Smaller mountain regions include the MacDonnell and Musgrave ranges (in central Australia), the Hamersley Range (northwest), Darling Range (southwest), Flinders Ranges (south-central), and the mountains of Tasmania. The longest rivers – the Murray and Darling – flow in the southeast.

The Darling, Australia's longest river, is dry along most of its course in winter. In summer, its waters flow into the Murray, Australia's longest permanently flowing river.

WATER AND POWER

Australia's biggest water-saving project is the Snowy Mountains Scheme, begun in 1949. It has been called one of the "Seven Wonders of the Engineering World."

- **Water from melting snows in the Snowy Mountains flows along aqueducts and tunnels to 16 dams for storage.**

- **The water is then led along other aqueducts and tunnels into the Murray and Murrumbidgee rivers to irrigate farmland in Victoria and New South Wales.**

- **Seven hydroelectric plants at the dams use water power to make electricity.**

Water is plentiful in Tasmania. The island's wild and rugged mountains, river valleys, and tranquil lakes create some of the most beautiful scenery in Australia.

A land lacking water

Australia is so dry that many rivers and most lakes dry up for months – or years – at a time. The only permanent lakes have been artificially created, such as Lake Argyle in Western Australia and Lake Gordon in Tasmania. Dry lakes or playas fill with water only after heavy rain. The largest of these dry lakes are in South Australia. They include Lake Eyre and Lake Torrens.

Underground water is fairly plentiful. Much of this is artesian water, trapped deep underground. The water is under such great pressure that it gushes to the surface when a well is dug. On many large cattle and sheep farms, artesian wells supply all the drinking water for the animals.

Facts about Australia

Area: 2,978,147 sq mi. (7,713,364 sq km) including 26,000 sq mi. (67,800 sq km) for the island of Tasmania.

Greatest distances (mainland): east-west – 2,475 mi. (3,983 km); north-south – 1,950 mi. (3,138 km).

Coastline: 17,366 mi. (27,948 km) including 779 mi. (1,254 km) for Tasmania.

Highest point: Mount Kosciusko, 7,310 ft. (2,228 m) above sea level.

Lowest point: Lake Eyre, 52 ft. (16 m) below sea level.

Longest rivers: Darling, 1,702 mi. (2,740 km) and Murray, 1,609 mi. (2,589 km).

Population: 18,058,000 (estimated to rise to 19,268,000 by 2001).

The Darling Downs is a fertile plain known as the "granary of Queensland" because crops thrive in its rich soil.

Australia's federation

Australia is a federation of six states – New South Wales, Victoria, Tasmania, South Australia, Western Australia, and Queensland. There are two mainland territories – the Australian Capital Territory and the Northern Territory. Australia also has eight external territories. The two states with the largest population are New South Wales and Victoria in the southeast.

The Three Sisters, part of the Blue Mountains west of Sydney, are a popular tourist attraction in New South Wales.

BELLOWING BUNYIPS!

According to the Australian Aborigines, the bunyip is an Australian animal that lives in water holes. But the bunyip is probably mythical. Scholars point out that Aborigines first mentioned bunyips about the same time that European settlers brought cattle into Australia. They suggest that the Aborigines became alarmed at the bellowing of cattle caught in the mud near water holes. However, several Europeans claim to have sighted bunyips at such places as Lake George and Lake Illawarra in New South Wales.

DESERT FLOWERS

Wildflowers grow even in desert areas of Australia.

- The seeds of desert flowers lie buried in the ground until rain brings them to life.
- Then, for a short time, the desert is carpeted with flowers of every imaginable color.

Wet and dry

Deserts cover about one-third of Australia. The four major deserts are the Simpson Desert, the Gibson Desert, the Great Sandy Desert, and the Great Victoria Desert. The Gibson Desert is stony, while the others are vast expanses of swirling sands.

By contrast, the east coast of Queensland is the country's wettest area. In Australia, snow falls only in Tasmania and the Australian Alps, where the temperature stays below freezing for more than a day at a time.

Most Australians enjoy warm summers and mild winters. Winter in Australia lasts from June to August; summer, the hottest and driest season, lasts from December to February. In tropical northern Australia, it is warm or hot all year round, but there are two seasons – one wet and one dry.

Plant life in Australia depends on the rainfall. The interior, which is dry most of the year, bursts into bloom after heavy rains (below). Rain forests along the northeast coast receive plenty of rain and stay green all year (below, right).

Golden wheat (below) stretches into the distance in Western Australia, the largest of Australia's six states. Although much of the land here is too dry for farming, wheat is a successful crop in the southwest.

Ancient rocks in Australia form dramatic landscapes, and contain valuable minerals.

The rock that glows

Ayers Rock rises 1,142 feet (348 meters) from the sandy plains southwest of Alice Springs in the Northern Territory. It is a 5-mile (8-kilometer) walk around the base of this huge outcrop of sandstone. Ayers Rock glows red during sunrise and sunset.

The rock was named for Sir Henry Ayers, premier of South Australia when it was visited by the explorer William Gosse in 1878. In 1985, the land around the rock was returned to its traditional Aboriginal owners, the Mutijula people. They turned over the management of the Uluru National Park to the Australian federal government on a 99-year lease.

Ayers Rock is called *Uluru* ("great pebble") by the Aborigines. Many of the caves inside the huge rock are covered with rock paintings made by Aboriginal artists long ago.

The Twelve Apostles are unusual rock formations near Port Campbell on the southern coast of Victoria.

The Olgas, 30 gigantic dome-shaped rocks, tower above the landscape near Ayers Rock. They are made of more than one type of rock, hence their striking color.

Hamersley Range, in Western Australia, contains one-tenth of the world's known resources of iron, as well as other minerals, including asbestos, copper, manganese, and tin.

WHEN DINOSAURS ROAMED

Some Australian rocks were formed over 3,000 million years ago.

● **About 600 million years ago, central Australia was covered by a shallow sea.**

● **Dinosaurs roamed Australia during the Jurassic Period, from 180 million to 130 million years ago.**

● **At one time all the earth's continents were part of one huge land mass. Then, about 200 million years ago, Australia broke away. From then on, Australian animals developed differently from those on other continents.**

PLACES TO SEE

Australia has many natural wonders. Wildlife areas worth a visit include:

Southwest National Park (Tasmania). Some of the park's Huon pines (tall evergreens) may be 3,000 years old.

Kakadu National Park (Northern Territory). Here you can see a fascinating world of vast swamplands, steep cliffs, Aboriginal rock paintings, water buffaloes, crocodiles, and water birds.

Kangaroo Island (South Australia). In Flinders Chase National Park, native Australian wildlife thrives. Rabbits, foxes, and other European animals were never introduced onto Kangaroo Island as they were on the mainland.

Dandenong Ranges (Victoria). These forested hills southeast of Melbourne are rich in tree ferns, and exotic birdlife including kookaburras and lyrebirds. Take the hiking trails to explore them.

GO DIG FOR OPALS

Coober Pedy and Andamooka are opal-mining centers in South Australia. Visitors with a permit may dig for opals. To escape the heat, many miners' homes are built underground.

Across Australia

Australia is a land of enormous distances. It is also one of the most urbanized countries – a nation of city dwellers.

City folk

Well over 80 per cent of all Australians live in towns and cities, compared with only about 13 per cent in rural areas. About 70 per cent of Australia's people live in cities of more than 100,000 population.

Cities in Australia have changed since the 1950's with the construction of modern high-rise buildings. The courtyard of the M.L.C. Centre, an office complex in Sydney, is shown here.

A HERO OF AVIATION

Brisbane-born Sir Charles Kingsford Smith (1897-1935) was a pioneer flier.

- In 1928, Kingsford Smith and three crewmen made the first flight across the Pacific Ocean from the United States to Australia in an aircraft called *The Southern Cross.*

- He also made the first nonstop flight across Australia, and the first flight across the Tasman Sea between Australia and New Zealand.

- Kingsford Smith and his co-pilot Thomas Pethybridge disappeared in 1935 while attempting a record flight from Britain to Australia.

Sydney's airport is one of Australia's eight international airports. It is named after Australia's greatest aviation pioneer, Sir Charles Kingsford Smith.

A lonely outback road seems to stretch as far as the eye can see.

Out in the bush

Australians call the remote countryside the *bush*. The term *outback* refers specifically to the interior.

The outback consists mainly of open countryside, including grazing land. It can be lonely. People living on isolated cattle or sheep farms (known as "stations") may be 100 miles (160 kilometers) from the nearest town. Some farm families use a light airplane for their trips to town.

Nearly every family in Australia owns a car. Paved roads link the state capitals, but most roads in the outback are dirt roads. Air and rail transportation help span the vast distances across Australia.

On the rails

Some of the world's longest rail journeys are taken across Australia. Passengers on the *Indian Pacific* spend nearly three days enjoying the train's comforts as they cross 2,447 miles (3,938 kilometers) of barren landscape between Perth and Sydney. The world's longest stretch of straight track – 297 miles (478 kilometers) – heads across the middle of the Nullarbor Plain. The *Trans Australian* train from Adelaide to Perth also uses this line.

Railway staff and their families look forward to the weekly *Tea and Sugar* train with on-board medical and supermarket facilities, as well as a movie theater!

CAMEL TRAIN

Afghan traders once drove teams of camels across central Australia. The name of the *Ghan* train is a reminder of those days. This train links Adelaide to Alice Springs, a distance of 960 miles (1,544 kilometers).

A train crosses the Barron Gorge in northern Queensland. Queensland has Australia's biggest state rail system.

EAU CLAIRE DIST

Australia's Wonderful Reef

The Great Barrier Reef is one of the wonders of the world and Australia's unique natural attraction.

Biggest in the world

The Great Barrier Reef off the northeast coast of Australia is the biggest coral reef in the world. It stretches for about 1,250 miles (2,010 kilometers) and includes about 400 different kinds of corals.

The reef is also the world's largest marine park, protected by the Australian government. From Gladstone and ports to the north, boats carry visitors to the island resorts. Sunshine, sandy beaches, fascinating wildlife, and ideal conditions for water sports make the region a popular tourist destination.

A diver explores the reef. About 1,500 kinds of fish live around the coral, so there is plenty to see! Many other undersea animals make their homes on the reef, including crabs, clams, sea urchins, starfish, sea cucumbers, sponges, and sea turtles.

REEF FACTS

- Most of the Great Barrier Reef developed over the last 2 million years, though experts suggest that parts of it are much older.

- Mountain ranges cut off from the mainland by the rising sea formed high, rocky continental islands, such as Magnetic Island and the islands of the Whitsunday group.

- The small islands, known as coral cays, are much lower than the mountain top islands, but some are covered with dense forests.

The Great Barrier Reef stretches along the Queensland coast from Gladstone beyond Cape York and north to New Guinea. This amazing series of coral formations includes thousands of small islands and many individual reefs.

Corals flourish in the clear, sunlit seas around the reef, providing shelter for its animals.

Australia's Plants

With hundreds of different kinds of trees and thousands of wildflowers, Australia has an amazingly rich plant life.

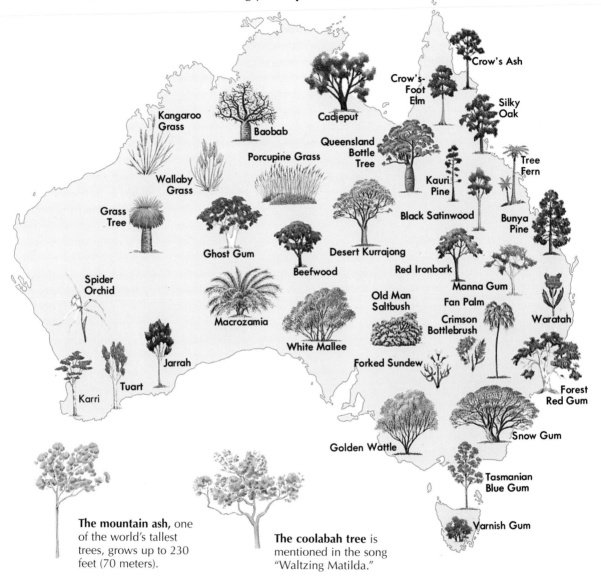

Crow's Ash

Crow's-Foot Elm

Silky Oak

Kangaroo Grass

Baobab

Cadjeput

Queensland Bottle Tree

Tree Fern

Porcupine Grass

Wallaby Grass

Kauri Pine

Grass Tree

Black Satinwood

Bunya Pine

Ghost Gum

Desert Kurrajong

Red Ironbark

Spider Orchid

Beefwood

Manna Gum

Old Man Saltbush

Fan Palm

Macrozamia

Crimson Bottlebrush

Waratah

White Mallee

Jarrah

Forked Sundew

Tuart

Karri

Forest Red Gum

Snow Gum

Golden Wattle

Tasmanian Blue Gum

Varnish Gum

The mountain ash, one of the world's tallest trees, grows up to 230 feet (70 meters).

The coolabah tree is mentioned in the song "Waltzing Matilda."

The plant landscape

Two kinds of native trees, the acacia and the eucalyptus, dominate Australia's landscape. Palms grow, too, as well as trees that look like palms (grass trees and macrozamias), and a few cone-bearing needleleaf trees such as kauri pine and bunya pine. Shrubs called saltbushes grow in dry areas; their salty leaves provide feed for livestock.

Plants of Australia. This picture-map shows some of the unusual and interesting plants of Australia. Many of these, such as wallaby grass and golden wattles, grow in other areas besides those shown, but forest trees are found only in the moist coastal regions.

Eucalyptus trees thrive all over mainland Australia and Tasmania.

Wattles and gums

Australians call acacia trees "wattles." There are about 700 species of these trees, which bear their seeds in pods. Many wattles have brilliant flowers.

Eucalyptus trees are found throughout Australia. Many Australians call them "gum trees" because their fruits ooze a sticky gum. More than 500 kinds grow in Australia, including the very tall mountain ash. Smooth-barked gum trees shed their bark every year.

The scarlet banksia grows in the south-west of Australia.

The baobab tree grows in northern Western Australia. Its bulbous trunk can measure 33 ft. (10 meters) around.

WHAT MAKES SCRIBBLY GUMS?

Scribbly gums are found on the eastern coast of Australia. The satiny-white bark of these trees is marked with what look like scribbles. The marks are made by the caterpillars of tiny moths that burrow under the bark and eat the soft new growth. The scars they leave are the scribbles!

The bottle tree's trunk looks like a bottle. This tree grows in dry regions of northeast Australia.

Birds of Australia

The brilliantly colorful birds of Australia include parrots and cockatoos, giant eagles, and birds of paradise, as well as large flightless birds.

A unique mixture

The world's only black swans come from Australia, as do the emu and cassowary – large flightless birds. In all, Australia has 700 or so species of birds, including about 60 kinds of cockatoos, parakeets, and other parrots.

Birds of paradise, bowerbirds, honeyeaters, fairy wrens, and lyrebirds are found only in Australia and surrounding islands. Rare birds include several species of parrot, freckled duck, malleefowl, and the noisy scrub bird – a ground-living bird from Western Australia with a loud and varied call.

Some bird species common elsewhere are thinly represented. Australia has no woodpeckers, only one crane (the brolga), and one stork (the jabiru).

The wedge-tailed eagle is one of the world's largest eagles. It feeds on mammals, birds, and reptiles – and will even swoop on a young kangaroo.

The laughing kookaburra is a kingfisher that sometimes catches fish, but usually eats reptiles, birds, small mammals, and insects. The kookaburra's loud, harsh call is a familiar sound in residential areas.

The cassowary is one of Australia's two large flightless birds; the other is the emu. The cassowary lives in forests, butting through undergrowth with the bony helmet on its head.

Foreign arrivals

Many birds, including blackbirds, pigeons, starlings, and sparrows, were introduced by settlers from Europe. Today, some of these imports are regarded as pests.

The brolga is a crane found in most coastal parts of Australia, except the southwest and southeast. Brolgas live in pairs or in flocks on plains or in swamps.

The superb lyrebird is one of Australia's most unusual birds. The male shows off its elaborate tail feathers, which are arranged like the ancient stringed musical instrument called a lyre.

Budgerigars are small, colorful parakeets. In the wild, they fly in flocks. Domestic-bred budgerigars are entertaining pets.

The white cockatoo uses its powerful curved bill to feed on seeds, nuts, and fruits. It is a common house pet and, like the budgerigar, makes a good talker.

Black swans live on lakes, rivers, and swamps. This graceful bird is completely black except for white patches on the wings and its red bill and eyes. The young, called cygnets, become black as adults.

Beautiful ... and Deadly

Many of Australia's animals are beautiful to look at, but some are best avoided!

Australia is rich in insects and other invertebrates, such as spiders. Most of these creatures are harmless, but some are venomous.

Snakes and other reptiles

Australia has about 140 species of snakes – and most of them are poisonous! The taipan and the tiger snake are among the deadliest reptiles in the world. None of the country's 370 species of lizards are poisonous, however.

The taipan, among the world's deadliest snakes, is Australia's largest and most feared venomous snake. Taipans, found in Queensland and in Arnhem Land in the Northern Territory, can grow to nearly 10 feet (3 meters) long.

The Australian frilled lizard frightens off its enemies by opening its mouth with a loud hiss and unfolding a large frill around its head. It can bite, but is otherwise harmless.

Brown snakes of eastern Australia are poisonous, with extremely potent venom. Fortunately, their fangs and venom glands are small, so victims of a brown snake's bite have a fair chance of recovery. Brown snakes grow up to 6 feet (1.8 meters) long.

Carpet snakes, which grow up to 13 feet (4 meters) long, are nonpoisonous. These snakes are widespread in Australia's coastal rain forests and inland deserts. They eat small mammals.

CROCS AT SEA!

Watch out if you go swimming in northern Australia. Sharks are not the only fearsome animals in Australian waters. You might meet the giant saltwater crocodile – the largest living reptile. The giant crocs are found in the ocean from Malaysia and Indonesia south to Australia. They grow up to 16 feet (nearly 5 meters) long – and sometimes longer!

Cane toad

CATCH THAT TOAD!

The cane toad has become a serious pest. These large toads from tropical America were brought to Australia in 1935 to help control beetles that attack sugar cane.

● Besides beetles, however, cane toads also eat frogs, lizards, snakes, mice, and small birds.

● The toads have few natural enemies. There are now so many in Australia that certain small native animals are threatened with extinction because the toads eat so many of them.

Creepy-crawlies

Australia is home to about 150,000 kinds of insects, as well as 1,600 kinds of spiders and other creepy-crawly creatures. Some of these have poisonous bites or stings, but most are harmless.

The green tree frog uses the sticky pads on its toes to climb trees.

The Ulysses or **Mountain Blue** is one of the many beautiful butterflies that flutter around Australia.

Redback spiders are related to black widow spiders and highly poisonous. The female has a red or orange mark on her body. Redback and funnel-web spiders are the only spiders known to have caused deaths in Australia.

21

Marvelous Mammals

Australia's most famous native animals are the marsupials, including kangaroos, koalas, wallabies, and wombats.

What's a marsupial?

Marsupials are mammals that give birth to tiny, poorly developed babies that mature in a pouch on the mother's abdomen. Australia has about 150 kinds of marsupials.

The red kangaroo is one of the largest kangaroos. Like all kangaroos, it carries its young in a pouch.

The kangaroo family

About 50 kinds of kangaroos live in Australia. Some, like the red and gray kangaroos, are as big as antelope. Others are as small as cats.

There are three main groups of the kangaroo family. Reds, grays, euros or wallaroos, wallabies, and tree kangaroos form one group. Rat kangaroos (including bettongs and potoroos) form the second group. Musky rat kangaroos, which make up the third group, have five toes on the hind foot, instead of the usual four.

KANGAROO FACTS

- A large kangaroo can hop over a fence as high as 6 feet (1.8 meters).

- A newborn baby kangaroo, or joey, is only 1 inch (2.5 centimeters) long.

- The joey stays in its mother's pouch for about 6 months.

- Until a joey is about 8 months old, it scrambles back into its mother's pouch at any sign of danger.

Kangaroos bound along on their powerful back legs, using their long tails to keep balanced.

A mother koala carries her babies on her back. The cub spends its first six months in the mother's pouch and the next six months on her back. Koalas eat eucalyptus leaves.

What's a wallaby?

Wallabies are really just small kangaroos, though some "wallabies" are actually larger than some "kangaroos!" To further confuse things, the red-necked wallaby of eastern Australia is usually called a "kangaroo" in Tasmania.

Rock wallabies leap along cliff faces with the agility of goats. Pademelons are small wallabies that live in wet, forested areas. Among the most famous wallabies are the quokkas, which are about the size of hares and have short tails. Much of the basic research on kangaroos was carried out on quokkas.

Tree climbers

Tree kangaroos are found in the rain forests of northern Queensland. They live in the trees, leaping from branch to branch. Tree kangaroos have short back legs and, like some monkeys, prehensile tails that grip onto branches.

The dingo is Australia's wild dog. Dingoes hunt wallabies and sometimes kill sheep, but if they are caught as puppies, dingoes make good pets.

Wombats are burrowing animals related to koalas. Wombats eat leaves and grass. They use only a third as much energy and water as most other animals, and this helps them survive on a poor diet of dry, tough plants. Two kinds of wombats live in Australia – the common wombat (shown here) and the hairy-nosed wombat.

Numbats live only in the southwestern corner of Australia. This numbat is searching for termites on top of a termite mound. It catches the insects with its long, sticky tongue. The numbat is an unusual marsupial because the female has no pouch.

Some of the world's oddest mammals live in Australia – flying opossums, egg-laying mammals, marsupial anteaters, and ratlike marsupials!

Two of a kind

The platypus and the echidna are two of Australia's most interesting – and most peculiar – animals. All other mammals give birth to live young, but not these two. Instead, they lay eggs that have a leathery shell. After an incubation period, the eggs hatch. These two primitive mammals, which are known as monotremes, are found only in Australia, Tasmania, and New Guinea.

Duckbill swimmer

The platypus lives beside streams. It is often called the duckbill because its snout resembles a duck's bill. The platypus uses its bill to scoop up worms, small shellfish, and other animals from stream beds. It has no teeth but crushes its food with horny pads on the back of its jaws.

The platypus lives alone in its burrow, except when females are rearing young. Female platypuses lay up to three eggs, which hatch after about 10 days. The young stay in a nest of leaves and grass inside the burrow for about four months, feeding on their mother's milk.

The platypus uses its broad, flat tail and webbed feet for swimming.

Toothless digger

The echidna is also known as the spiny anteater. It lives on insects, which it licks up with its long tongue since it has no teeth. The echidna has coarse, brown hair and many sharp spines on its back and sides. When danger threatens, these strange animals dig burrows with their strong front claws and then hide inside until it is safe to come out.

Each year, the echidna lays one egg which hatches in a pouch that forms on the female's belly. The young echidna stays in the pouch for several weeks, nourished by its mother's milk.

The **feather-tail glider** is a tiny opossum about 3 inches (7 centimeters) long. The smallest flying marsupial, it lives in eucalyptus forests, where it feeds on insects and nectar. Also known as the *pygmy glider*, this tiny marsupial glides through the air using folds of skin and its featherlike tail as a parachute.

The echidna is no beauty, but scientists find it fascinating.

The bandicoot, which looks like a rat, is a small marsupial that lives on insects, spiders, and worms. Most bandicoots live in forests, but one species, the *bilby,* is found in deserts.

Australians All

The first Australians were the Aborigines. In 1788, Britain established a prison colony in New South Wales. Free settlers followed and since then millions of immigrants, from many countries, have made new lives in Australia.

Nine out of ten Australians are of European descent, chiefly British and Irish. But you'll also meet Italians, Greeks, Germans, Dutch, Chinese, and Indochinese, as well as people from countries of the Middle East, the Indian subcontinent, and Indonesia. Aborigines make up about 1 per cent of the population today.

The Aborigines are descendants of Australia's first settlers, who migrated from Asia thousands of years ago. These Aboriginal children with their teacher are at school in Queensland.

Sovereign Hill, in Ballarat, Victoria, shows tourists what the city looked like at the height of the gold rush in the 1850's. Visitors can pan for gold, and see huts and tents like those in which the miners lived.

An Oriental food shop in Sydney. Increasing numbers of Asians, including Chinese, have settled in Australia since the 1970's.

EATING AND DRINKING

● Australians enjoy barbecues and picnics, and eat a lot of meat.

● Italian, Greek, and Asian foods are also popular.

● Tea is Australia's favorite hot drink, though coffee drinking is growing steadily.

● Beer is the most popular alcoholic drink.

Speak Australian

Australian English includes many British terms. For example, Australians say *lift*, not *elevator*, and fill their cars with *petrol*, not *gasoline*.

British settlers in Australia sometimes used familiar words to describe the unfamiliar animals and plants they saw. They gave the name *magpie* to a bird that looks like the British magpie, but is not a relative at all. They also borrowed words from the Aborigines, such as *kangaroo* and *koala*.

Pioneer settlers in the interior of Australia invented their own words. Large farms became known as *stations*, their owners as *squatters*. A herd of animals is a *mob*, and wild horses are *brumbies*.

Cairns in tropical Queensland, where tourists can hire boats to explore the Great Barrier Reef, is very different from the industrial towns and small villages that many British and Irish immigrants left behind to make the long journey to Australia.

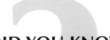

DID YOU KNOW?

Australia's most famous song is "Waltzing Matilda," probably written by Banjo Paterson (1864-1941), who wrote many bush ballads about shearers, drovers, and squatters. The song's title does not refer either to a dance or a woman. A matilda is a blanket roll. "To waltz matilda" means to tramp the roads.

Famous Australians

Australians have distinguished themselves in many fields. The people listed and pictured here are all outstanding Australians.

Australia's many tennis champions include Rod Laver. This dynamic left-hander from Rockhampton in Queensland won all four major world singles titles in 1962 and again in 1969. He was the first player to achieve the *grand slam* twice.

Joan Sutherland thrilled opera audiences with her singing. She is seen here (second from right) in a scene from *The Daughter of the Regiment,* by the Italian composer Donizetti.

MEDICAL FIRSTS

- Australian-born Howard Florey, later Lord Florey (1898-1968), helped develop the antibiotic penicillin, and shared the 1945 Nobel Prize for medicine with Sir Alexander Fleming and Ernst Chain.

- Sir Macfarlane Burnet (1899-1985), a Nobel prizewinner in 1960, suggested the possibility of organ transplants in 1949, and pioneered techniques for skin grafting.

- William McBride (1927-) achieved world prominence in 1961 by discovering that the drug thalidomide caused deformities in unborn children.

AUSTRALIA ROCKS

Australia's international pop music stars include the Bee Gees, Olivia Newton-John, Kylie Minogue, Jason Donovan, AC/DC, Men at Work, and INXS.

Sir Robert Menzies was Australia's longest-serving prime minister, holding office from 1939 to 1941, and again from 1949 to 1966.

ACE AUSSIES

Any list of famous Australians of modern times would include these men and women.

Dame Judith Anderson (1898-1992), actress

Richie Benaud (1930-), cricketer, never lost a test series as Australian captain

Neville Bonner (1918-), first Aboriginal member of Parliament

Jack Brabham (1926-), three times world Grand Prix car-racing champion (1959, 1960, 1966)

Sir Donald Bradman (1908-), probably cricket's greatest batsman

Evonne Cawley (1951-), twice Wimbledon tennis champion

Ron Clarke (1937-), one of the greatest runners in history

Margaret Court (1942-), tennis player, only player to achieve the *grand slam* in doubles,1963, and in singles, 1970

Herb Elliott (1938-), runner of 17 under-4-minute miles, Olympic gold medal winner,1960

Dawn Fraser (1937-), swimmer who won gold medals at the 1956, 1960, and 1964 Olympics

Malcolm Fraser (1930-), prime minister from 1975 to 1983

Mel Gibson (1956-), actor, star of *Mad Max, Braveheart*, and other films

Kevin Gilbert (1933-), Aboriginal dramatist

Shane Gould (1956-), swimmer, won three golds, one silver, one bronze medal at 1972 Olympics

Germaine Greer (1939-), scholar and writer, leader in the women's movement

Janine Haines (1945-), first Australian woman to lead a political party (the Australian Democrats, in 1986)

Rolf Harris (1930-), entertainer and singer

Bob Hawke (1929-), prime minister from 1983 to 1991

Paul Hogan (1940-), actor, star of *Crocodile Dundee* (1986)

Lew Hoad (1934-1994), tennis player

John Howard (1939-), prime minister from 1996

Barry Humphries (1934-), entertainer who created the character of Dame Edna Everage

Cathy Freeman (1973-) was the first Aboriginal athlete to represent Australia in the Olympic Games. She won a silver medal at 400 meters in 1996.

Paul Keating (1944-), prime minister from 1991 to 1996

Thomas Keneally (1935-), author of *Schindler's Ark*

Dennis Lillee (1949-), cricketer who took 355 wickets in 70 tests

Stuart Mackenzie (1936-), rowing champion

Sir Charles Mackerras (1925-), orchestral conductor

Keith Michell (1928-), actor

Rupert Murdoch (1931-), media tycoon (since 1985 a U.S. citizen)

Albert Namatjira (1902-1959), Aboriginal painter

Sir Sidney Nolan (1917-1992), painter

Greg Norman (1955-), golfer nicknamed "The Great White Shark"

Lionel Rose (1948-), world bantamweight boxing champion in 1968

Ken Rosewall (1934-), tennis player who won all major titles except Wimbledon

Peter Weir (1938 -), film director

Patrick White (1912-1990), writer, winner of 1973 Nobel Prize for literature.

New and Old

Australia is a land of fast-changing cities. Modern high-rise buildings and spreading residential areas create the city landscapes, along with reminders of Australia's past.

Canberra, the capital

Australia's national capital is Canberra, in the Australian Capital Territory (ACT). The capital was designed from a plan drawn up by the U.S. landscape architect Walter Burley Griffin. Work began in 1913, but government business was still done in Melbourne until after World War II (1939-1945).

Parliament House in Canberra was opened in 1988 as part of Australia's bicentennial celebrations. The building stands on a hill behind the old Parliament House established in 1927. The national Parliament – the Senate and the House of Representatives – meets in this impressive building.

CAPITAL SHOWCASE

Places to visit in Canberra include:

- **The Australian National Gallery, and the Canberra Theatre Centre**
- **The Australian National University**
- **The Institute of Anatomy (with its museums of Aboriginal culture and Australian plants)**
- **The Royal Australian Mint**
- **The Botanic Gardens and National Herbarium**
- **Government House, official residence of the governor general.**

The Australian War Memorial in Canberra was completed in 1941. Lake Burley Griffin was created in the 1960's, and Lake Ginninderra in the 1970's.

Old Australia

Many reminders of pioneer days remain in Australia. Even in modern Canberra you can visit Blundell's Farmhouse, a stone cottage built in 1858, and Lanyon, a farm dating from 1835.

Visitors to Kalgoorlie in Western Australia can see buildings that date from the gold rush days. They can stroll along a street little changed since 1893, when more than 1,400 miners arrived in the town within one week, all hoping to strike it rich by finding gold. Few of them did.

Older-style buildings are preserved in many Australian towns and cities. Duntroon, a historic building in Canberra, was built by Robert Campbell in 1833. It is now part of the Royal Military College.

Kalgoorlie is at the heart of Australia's major gold and nickel fields. The town, which grew rapidly after gold was discovered in 1893, is famous for the historic buildings that line its main street.

Cities of Australia

St. Peter's Cathedral, Adelaide, is built in traditional style. Adelaide, capital of South Australia, is known for its many beautiful churches.

Adelaide, Darwin, and Hobart – three very different cities – are the state capitals of South Australia, the Northern Territory, and Tasmania.

City of churches and parks

Adelaide, the capital of South Australia, is often called the City of Churches because it has so many of these beautiful buildings. It is also the largest city in South Australia, with just over a million people. Adelaide hosts the Australian Grand Prix car race and the Adelaide Festival of arts, which is held every two years.

The city was planned in 1837 by Colonel William Light, first surveyor general of South Australia. His plan provided wide streets, squares, and parklands around the central area. Visitors to Adelaide also enjoy the beauty of its coastline and hills, and its mild climate. The city has a flourishing economy, employing about 73 per cent of South Australia's workers.

Darwin is the capital of the Northern Territory and its major deepwater port.

CITY FACTS

- **Darwin is named in honor of British naturalist Charles Darwin. Its harbor was first sighted in 1839 by the crew of H.M.S. *Beagle*, a ship on which Darwin had sailed in 1831-36.**

- **The Torrens River flows through Adelaide, providing attractive terraced hillside walks as well as boating and fishing.**

- **Hobart's Regatta, held since 1838, includes a wide range of water sports.**

Hobart, capital of Tasmania, lies along the beautiful Derwent River.

Cosmopolitan Darwin

Darwin is the capital of the Northern Territory. About 78,000 people, most of European descent, live in the city. But many residents have Aboriginal, Chinese, Malay, or Filipino ancestry.

In 1974, Darwin was devastated by Cyclone Tracy, and the city was almost completely rebuilt. It is an important transportation center. The Stuart Highway links the city with Alice Springs, and with other major highways. Darwin also has an international airport and a busy deepwater port for shipping, as well as military bases, including a naval port.

Historic Hobart

Hobart, capital of Tasmania, has about 181,000 people living in the metropolitan area. Its many places of historic interest include Battery Point, with its fine early houses, and the Victorian Theatre Royal, built in 1834. The city's port has modern cargo-handling facilities. Hobart is also the chocolate capital of Australia. The country's largest cocoa and confectionery factory is at Claremont.

Brisbane and Perth stand on opposite sides of Australia. Both cities are impressive state capitals, with a wide range of arts, educational, sports, and commercial activities.

THE NAME'S THE SAME

British visitors to Brisbane feel right at home. Tourist maps list such familiar place names as Ascot, Windsor, Newmarket, Chatsworth, and Holland Park.

Queensland's capital

About 1.3 million people live in metropolitan Brisbane, the largest city in the state of Queensland. The city, on the Brisbane River, is Australia's busiest river port.

Thousands of commuters travel daily into the two main business districts – the city with its tall office blocks, banks, shops, and entertainments; and the smaller Fortitude Valley district. Also in Fortitude Valley is Brisbane's Chinatown development, built in the 1980's.

The city's large areas of parkland and bush include the Old Botanic Gardens and Brisbane Forest Park. Brisbane is a lively cultural and sports center. The magnificent QEII stadium, opened at Nathan in 1975, hosted the 1982 Commonwealth Games.

Brisbane's modern skyline forms an impressive background to the Brisbane River as it flows through the city's main business area.

Perth stands along the Swan River. The city has many fine modern buildings and well-planned, tree-lined streets.

THE FREMANTLE DOCTOR

During Perth's long, dry summers, searing hot winds sometimes blow from the inland Gibson Desert. When the city is not basking in a heat wave, a cooling sea breeze known as the Fremantle Doctor blows in each afternoon.

Perth stands alone

On a plain near the warm Indian Ocean lies Perth, the business center of Western Australia. More than 1 million people live here in what is probably the world's most isolated large city. Its nearest large neighbor is Adelaide, 1,678 miles (2,700 kilometers) away. Fremantle is the port of Perth.

Many people think Perth is one of Australia's most beautiful cities, with its tree-lined streets and fine surfing beaches. The Swan and Canning rivers flow through the city, but water supply is a problem because Perth has hot, dry summers. Water is piped into the city from reservoirs in the Darling Range.

Perth's attractions include the 8,000-seat Entertainment Centre and the Concert Hall. The restored Old Women's Home, built in the 1850's, displays relics from Dutch ships wrecked off the west coast of Australia in the 1600's.

Old Brisbane houses were built on wooden stumps to protect them from termites and to provide a cool, shaded area under the house.

Sydney and Melbourne are the largest cities in Australia. Sydney is the capital of New South Wales. Melbourne is the capital of the neighboring state of Victoria.

Australia's largest city

Sydney is the gateway to Australia. Most visitors enter and leave the country through Australia's oldest and largest city, with a population of more than 3.5 million.

Sydney has a wonderful setting on a huge, deep harbor, called Port Jackson, or Sydney Harbour. Sights to see in Sydney include Bondi Beach, the Royal Botanic Gardens, Taronga Zoo, Sydney Harbour with its steel arch bridge, and the city's premier landmark – the spectacular Opera House built in 1973, with its roof of billowing "sails." Sydney was chosen to host the summer Olympic Games in the year 2000.

Sydney has one of the finest harbors in the world. The Sydney Harbour Bridge links the city's business district with the suburbs to the north. The Sydney Opera House can be seen to the left of the bridge.

GETTING AROUND

- **Sydney's subway was built in 1926 and its monorail in 1988. The Sydney Harbour Tunnel opened in 1992.**

- **Melbourne's tramcars provide convenient public transportation to the city's shopping malls.**

Victorians in Melbourne

Melbourne, once the nation's capital, is Australia's second largest city, with just over 3 million people. About 66 per cent of all Victorians live in Melbourne, which lies on the shores of the natural harbor of Port Phillip Bay. The Yarra River flows through the city, and supplies most of the city's water.

Melbourne is Australia's largest general-cargo port. The city also has about 30 per cent of Australia's manufacturing industry. It is home to the National Museum, the Science Museum, and the National Gallery. The Melbourne Cricket Ground is one of the biggest and most famous cricket grounds in the world.

Melbourne's skyline provides a dramatic contrast with modern high-rise buildings and the spires of a traditional cathedral.

PIONEER AUSTRALIAN HOME

Most Australians live in modern houses in city suburbs. The pioneers of the 1800's built timber-slab cottages like this one, preserved as an interesting relic of Australia's past.

Times change. An old picture of Sydney, painted by F. Halstead in 1863, shows Circular Quay in Sydney Cove. A convict colony was set up in Sydney Cove in 1788.

On the Farm

Most of Australia's farmland is dry grazing land – poor for crops but ideal for sheep. And Australia has a lot of sheep!

The world leader

Australia has more sheep than any other country in the world – more than 167 million. Not surprisingly, it is the world's largest producer and exporter of wool.

By far the most important sheep-raising state is New South Wales, with almost one-third of Australia's sheep. Western Australia and Victoria are next in importance.

The Merino rules

Of every 100 sheep in Australia, 75 are Merinos. This breed is of Spanish origin and is noted for its fine wool. About 20 of every 100 animals are crossbreds, mainly Border Leicesters crossed with Merinos, for the meat trade.

Sheep do well on the dry grazing land that covers much of Australia west of the Eastern Highlands. This picture shows sheep in South Australia.

Sheep on station

Some sheep farms are enormous stations with more than 25,000 sheep ranging across the dry grassland. Sheep farms in high-rainfall areas are smaller. Most sheep farmers also raise cattle and grow wheat.

SHEAR SPEED

In 1892, Jack Howe hand-sheared 321 Merinos in 7 hours, 40 minutes at Blackall in Queensland. This Australian record stood for 58 years, even though later shearers used mechanical shears.

A shearer at work, using power clippers. An expert can clip the wool from 200 or more sheep in a day. Sheep are sheared once a year, mainly between June and September.

DID EWE KNOW?

- In 1796 a few Merino sheep were shipped to Australia from South Africa. Captain John Macarthur bought three rams (males) and five ewes (females).

- Macarthur pioneered wool production in Australia and introduced more Merinos from King George III's flock in England.

- In 1807 the first shipload of fine wool was sent to England, where it sold for high prices.

The outback of Australia is mainly desert and dry grassland. Sheep and cattle stations are scattered like islands across this vast expanse of empty, open country.

Nearly all farms in the outback are cattle or sheep stations. These are often extremely isolated. It is a long way to the nearest town – and even to the next farm.

Life on a station

The largest stations cover more than 1,000 square miles (2,600 square kilometers). They are often 100 miles (160 kilometers) or more from the nearest town.

The outback has few paved roads, so journeys by car may be difficult or impossible. Some farm families get to town only a few times a year.

People on these isolated stations keep large stocks of food, clothing, fuel, and other necessities. They keep in touch with the outside world by radio, television, and computer.

In such rural communities, people help one another out in bad times. They also meet to enjoy traditional fairs, festivals, and sports competitions.

AUSTRALIAN FARMS GO FARTHER

Wave Hill cattle station in northern Australia covers an area of 6,000 square miles (15,500 square kilometers). That's bigger than the U.S. state of Connecticut!

Beef roads

Almost all Australian cattle go to market by road. The federal government built beef roads across northern Australia, on which beef trains move large numbers of cattle overland to saleyards. A beef train consists of a truck and two to six trailers.

Cattle are mustered, or rounded up, by riders before being taken on trucks to market. Mustering takes place once a year in remote areas. The riders, known as stockmen, include many Aborigines.

A road train leaves a dust trail as it crosses a dry region of Western Australia.

41

Golden wheat fields, such as these in New South Wales, are vital to Australia's prosperity. Australia sells huge quantities of wheat to China, Japan, and other Asian countries.

AUSTRALIA PRODUCES ...

- cattle, wheat, wool,
- sugar, barley, oats, rice, potatoes,
- chickens and eggs,
- cotton and vegetables.

Crops are grown on only about 5 per cent of Australia's farmland. But farmers using modern methods make the cropland highly productive.

Cereal giant

Australia's 45,000 wheat farms produce enough grain to make it the world's fifth largest wheat exporter. Wheat is very important to the country's economy. Most wheat farms also raise livestock, and grow such other grains as barley, oats, and sorghum. The two chief wheat-growing states are Western Australia and New South Wales.

Lack of water is a problem in much of Australia. Wind pumps on the Eyre Peninsula in South Australia raise underground water through boreholes for irrigation. Irrigation makes it possible for farmers to grow wheat and oats.

Barossa Valley, near Adelaide in South Australia, is famous for its vineyards and wineries.

Australia's wines

The cooler southerly quarter of Australia produces most of the country's wines. The regions for premium wines include the Hunter Valley and Mudgee (New South Wales); Coonawarra and Barossa Valley (South Australia); Yarra Valley and Great Western (Victoria), and Margaret River and Mount Barker-Frankland (Western Australia).

Tropical and fruit farming

Farms on the east coast of Queensland grow sugar cane, bananas, pineapples, and other crops that thrive in a wet, tropical climate. Queensland produces about 95 per cent of the country's sugar. The state also ships winter vegetables by train to the southern states.

New South Wales and South Australia grow most of the country's oranges. Apples and pears are harvested nationwide.

WAR ON RABBITS

Australia's early settlers brought cats, deer, foxes, rabbits, and other animals with them. Some of these became pests.

- In 1859 a settler in Victoria released 24 rabbits. Within three years wild rabbits were a serious pest, eating farm crops and grass on grazing lands.

- In the 1950's, the introduction of the virus myxomatosis killed many rabbits, but their numbers are again increasing.

43

A Rich Land

Australia is rich in minerals, and the mining industry is a dominant factor in the economy. Mining also played an important part in the country's history.

What Australia sells abroad

In the 1950's, about 85 per cent of Australia's export income came from selling farm goods such as wool and wheat. Today, farm products account for only about 20 per cent of the country's export earnings. Minerals, raw materials, and manufactured products now make up 80 per cent of Australia's exports.

Gold is mined on the surface at the Kalgoorlie mine in Western Australia. Huge earth movers scrape away the surface to reach the deposits beneath.

LAND OF OPALS

Opal is a gemstone that contains a rainbow of colors. Most precious opals are mined in Australia.

- The most prized opals are black opals, which have a black, blue, or gray background. High-quality black opals are found in New South Wales.

- A huge opal called the Desert Flame of Andamooka was found in Australia in 1969. It weighed more than 6,800 grams.

Oil rigs in the Bass Strait tap huge reserves of oil and natural gas off the coast of Victoria.

AUSTRALIA MINES ...

Australia ranks first in world production of bauxite, industrial diamonds, and lead. Other minerals mined in Australia include copper, iron ore, manganese, nickel, tin, titanium, tungsten, uranium, zinc, and zircon.

Gas and oil

Natural gas and oil were discovered in the Bass Strait off the south coast of Victoria in the 1960's. Oil wells in the Bass Strait now supply most of the crude oil that Australians need for fuel. Natural gas has also been discovered off the northwest coast of Western Australia.

Coal and gold

Coal was found at Newcastle in New South Wales in 1791. The first coal mine opened in 1799, and Australia is now a major coal exporter. Lead and zinc mining began in the 1840's.

The great gold rushes of the 1850's brought settlers from all over the world to the gold fields of Bathurst, Ballarat, Bendigo, and Mount Alexander. Those days are long gone, but Australia is still the fifth largest producer of gold.

Iron and steel are made at Port Kembla in New South Wales, one of the fastest-growing industrial areas in Australia. Port Kembla produces almost two-thirds of Australia's pig iron and more than half its raw steel.

Australia's wealth has come chiefly from farming and mining. Manufacturing is less important, and service industries now employ the largest number of workers.

Sharing prosperity

Australia exports farm products and minerals to earn the income that most other developed countries make from exporting manufactured products. As a result, Australia's income is shared between farms, mines, and companies that process and distribute farm and mineral products, and many Australians have a high standard of living.

The Snowy Mountains Scheme's pipelines carry water from mountain streams to a series of dams and hydroelectric plants. The scheme provides energy and irrigation water.

AUSTRALIA MAKES ...

Processed foods, metals, motor vehicles, paper and printed materials, chemicals, textiles, clothing and shoes, and household appliances.

AUSTRALIA TRADES WITH ...
Japan, United States, United Kingdom, New Zealand, and Germany (its main trade partners).

AUSTRALIA EXPORTS ...
Coal, wheat, aluminum ore, iron ore, wool, beef, and petroleum products.

Fishing is a small but profitable industry. This trawler is netting prawns off the east coast. Prawns and other shellfish such as abalones, lobsters, oysters, and scallops, are sold overseas.

Manufacturing industries like this automobile plant in Sydney employ about 15 per cent of the labor force in Australia. New South Wales and Victoria have more than 60 per cent of the country's factories.

COMMUNICATING

- Nearly every household has a telephone. However, in the remotest parts of the outback, people rely on two-way radios.

- Almost all Australian families own one or more television sets and radios. The national daily paper is *The Australian*.

Imports and exports

Australia imports more manufactured goods than it exports. Yet its factories make most of the consumer goods, such as processed foods and household articles, that the people need. The nation imports goods such as factory machinery and construction equipment. However, Australia produces enough iron and steel to meet its needs.

Where people work

Hospitals, schools, banking, government agencies, stores, hotels, restaurants, and transportation services provide about two-thirds of the jobs in Australia.

Tourism is growing. About half of Australia's visitors come from places that are relatively close, such as New Zealand and other Pacific islands, and Japan.

A container ship docks in Melbourne's busy port. The city stands on the shores of Port Phillip Bay, the largest natural harbor in Victoria.

47

Australians Have Fun

Australians enjoy the outdoors, and sports are a national pastime. Australians start playing games at school and many continue to play them throughout life. People here just like having fun!

Taking to the water

Given their country's long ocean coastline and beautiful beaches, it's easy for Australians to take up swimming, boating, or rowing. Many people enjoy the thrills of surfing, especially in Queensland, New South Wales, and Western Australia.

Surfers enjoy the big waves at Wreck Bay in southern New South Wales.

The Gold Coast, south of Brisbane, has some of Queensland's best-known surfing beaches and many tourist hotels. This resort area includes Surfers Paradise and Coolangatta.

The Sydney-Hobart yacht race, an annual event, attracts competitors from many nations. The yachts leave Sydney on December 26 and race to Hobart, Tasmania.

Safe swimming

Thousands of trained volunteers patrol the beaches each weekend to keep them safe for bathers. These volunteers belong to surf lifesaving clubs. Club members use jet rescue powerboats and inflatables known as "rubber duckies." The Surf Life-Saving Association of Australia also operates rescue helicopters. Australia was the first country in the world to develop a surf lifesaving movement.

Surf boats provide spectacular action at surf carnivals. These boats were originally used for rescues, but are now more often seen racing or entertaining beach crowds.

SHARKS?

Most sharks in Australian waters are harmless scavengers. But there are some dangerous kinds – such as whalers, tiger sharks, and white sharks. Nets anchored offshore and air patrols protect popular beaches from sharks. Attacks on bathers are rare – more people die by drowning than are killed by sharks.

Popular team games include Australian football and cricket, which large crowds turn out to watch. Australia has also produced many world-famous runners, tennis players, golfers, and swimmers.

A sporting nation

The most popular team sports in Australia are cricket, Australian Rules football, Rugby League, Rugby Union, and soccer. You can enjoy the thrilling Melbourne Cup, the country's most famous horse race, and you can ski in Australia too.

Australian Rules football is fast and exciting. Players drive the ball back and forth with long kicks and quick hand passes and stop it with high catches called *marks*.

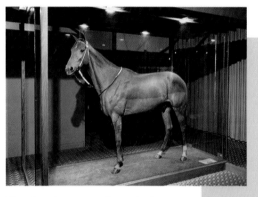

Phar Lap became a legend of the racetrack.

One of the most famous horses to win the Melbourne Cup was New Zealand-bred Phar Lap. Famed for his speed and spirit, he won Australia's greatest horse race in 1930.

- Between 1928 and 1932, Phar Lap won 36 of 50 races in Australia and one in the United States.

- Phar Lap died mysteriously in the United States in 1932.

- A taxidermist's lifelike model of the horse is displayed in the National Museum in Melbourne.

Skiers enjoy the snow that covers Mount Kosciusko and other peaks of the Australian Alps in winter.

Cricket in Australia draws big crowds, especially the one-day international games and test matches – particularly against England, Australia's oldest cricket rival.

CRICKET IN AUSTRALIA

- The first known cricket matches in Australia were played in Sydney in 1803.

- The first test (international) match between Australia and England took place at Melbourne in 1877. Australia won.

- The first Sheffield Shield competition was held in 1892-1893, when Victoria triumphed over New South Wales and South Australia.

AUSTRALIAN FOOTBALL FIRST

- Many experts believe that the first game of Australian Rules football was played in 1858 between boys from Scotch College, Melbourne, and Melbourne Grammar School.

- There were 40 players on each side, the game lasted almost 5 hours, and in that time Scotch College managed to score the only goal. The match was abandoned.

Cricket's Ashes

Since 1882, England and Australia have played cricket for *The Ashes*. This term was first used after Australia beat England in a match in London. An English newspaper jokingly lamented the death of English cricket, concluding "The body will be cremated and the ashes taken to Australia."

The following year an English team went to Australia and won. Some Australian women burned a cricket stump and put the ashes in a small urn, which they gave to the English captain. The urn is now displayed at Lord's cricket ground in London.

Football

Australia has its own football, a game of great pace and spectacle that developed from Gaelic (Irish) football. The first championship was held in 1906, and won by Victoria.

Both codes of Rugby football are also popular, and Australia's main international rivals in these games are Britain, France, New Zealand, and South Africa. Soccer is the fastest-growing team sport, and Australian stars also play for professional clubs in Europe.

Australia's Wallabies take on New Zealand's All Blacks at Rugby Union football. Games against the All Blacks arouse great excitement. Australia's national Rugby League team is called the Kangaroos.

Art and Architecture

Australia's unique combination of landscape, peoples, and cultural influences has created an art and architecture that is rich and varied.

Architecture

Architecture in Australia was strongly influenced by British styles until the 1900's. Many buildings were constructed in the Georgian and Victorian styles then popular in Britain, some of them with elaborate decoration. After passenger elevators were first installed in Australian buildings in the 1880's, cities shot skyward. Since the 1900's, North American architecture has had a growing influence. Today, dramatic modern buildings are found in every Australian city, and there are some fine buildings in the countryside too.

Sidney Myer Music Bowl in Melbourne has an eye-catching shell that provides superb sound for open-air summer concerts. The auditorium can seat 2,000 people beneath its canopy, with room for 20,000 more on the sloping lawns. The bowl was built in 1959, using a fund set up by Melbourne store owner Sidney Baevski Myer.

Music

Australian music is varied. Besides the state orchestras, there is the Australian Youth Orchestra, which gathers together some of the best young musicians. And opera has a strong tradition. Two of Australia's most famous international musicians – Dame Nellie Melba and Dame Joan Sutherland – have been opera singers. Other flourishing fields include country music, jazz, and pop.

The National Library of Australia in Canberra was established in 1960. It is the major research library in the country, with a collection of more than 2 million print volumes and over 3 million nonprint items.

Theater and cinema

The first theatrical show in Australia took place in 1789. It was a production of George Farquhar's play, *The Recruiting Officer,* performed by a cast of convicts in a mud hut on an improvised stage. A film of the Melbourne Cup horse race was made as early as 1896!

Today, theater and cinema are thriving in Australia. Each state capital has its own theater company, and networks of smaller professional and amateur groups take drama to schools and to people who live in out-of-the-way places.

Outstanding films have won Australia an international reputation. Their titles include *Picnic at Hanging Rock, Gallipoli,* and *My Brilliant Career,* and, in the 1990's, *Strictly Ballroom* and *Muriel's Wedding.*

Libraries

Each state capital has its own library of books, periodicals, newspapers, recordings, and other media. Important collections include the Mitchell Library, part of the State Library of New South Wales, which contains material relating to Australia and the Pacific area.

Adelaide Festival Theatre, built in 1973, is considered one of the finest theaters in Australia. Operas, ballets, concerts, plays, and films are staged there.

BLOW THE DIDGERIDOO

The didgeridoo, a kind of wooden trumpet played at Aboriginal religious ceremonies, is made from a straight, hollowed-out piece of wood, usually eaten up the center by termites. The didgeridoo's rhythmic, booming sound provides the background for a songman with his clapping stick.

The main concert hall of the Sydney Opera House is used regularly for orchestral concerts. The building is internationally famous as a unique architectural achievement of the modern age.

Artists and writers have both contributed to Australia's position in the modern world. Today's artists draw inspiration from the country's varied landscape, just as Aboriginal artists have always done.

Aboriginal art

Aboriginal art includes rock paintings and carvings, as well as paintings on sheets of bark. Two traditional art styles are *mimi* (stick-figure) *paintings* and *X-ray paintings*, in which illustrations of humans, animals, and fish show the internal organs and bones as well as flesh. Some rock-painting sites are *secret-sacred* (holy and hidden) and access to them is restricted.

A bark painting by a present-day Aboriginal artist. Traditional Aboriginal paintings are made on bark or rock, and they feature elaborate designs of human and animal figures.

St. John's Cathedral in Parramatta, Sydney, was begun in 1799 and is a good example of colonial architecture. Parramatta, the second oldest settlement in Australia, was founded on Nov. 2, 1788, by Governor Arthur Phillip.

TWELVE MODERN WRITERS

Australian literature has developed its own themes and styles. Leading writers since 1900 include the following (with examples of their work).

Miles Franklin *My Brilliant Career*

Xavier Herbert *Capricornia, Poor Fellow My Country*

Thomas Keneally *Schindler's Ark*

Hal Porter *Watcher on the Cast-Iron Balcony*

Roland Robinson *Black-feller, White-feller*

Christina Stead *The Man Who Loved Children*

Douglas Stewart *The Birdsville Track* (poetry)

Patrick White *Voss, The Eye of the Storm*

S.A. Wakefield *Bottersnikes and Gumbles* (for children)

David Williamson *Sons of Cain, The Emerald City* (plays)

Judith Wright *The Other Half, Alive* (poetry)

Patricia Wrightson *The Book of Wirrun* (for children)

54

Paintings of the 1800s showed how earlier generations of Australians enjoyed themselves. This 1855 picture shows people picnicking at a place called *Mrs. Macquarie's Chair*, near Sydney Cove.

A poster by the artist and writer Norman Lindsay (1879-1969) urged Australians to join the Army during World War I.

Modern painting

Australian artists have been influenced by trends in the international art world, as well as by the nature and history of their country. Many painters, including Sidney Nolan and Arthur Boyd, expressed striking personal visions of Australia. Other artists portrayed Australia through its myths and legends, in both abstract and figurative ways.

Glenrowan is a painting by Sidney Nolan (1917-1992), one of Australia's most distinguished artists. Sidney Nolan was born in Melbourne. He was knighted in 1981.

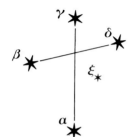

Southern Cross

Amazing Australia

Australia is full of surprises and good stories!

The flag of Australia

Australia's flag displays the *constellation* (group of stars) known as the Southern Cross, as well as the Union Jack and a large star that represents the states and territories. The Southern Cross is named for the outline of a cross formed by its four brightest stars. The brightest star is the one that lies farthest south, but people looking for it for the first time may find the Southern Cross difficult to pick out.

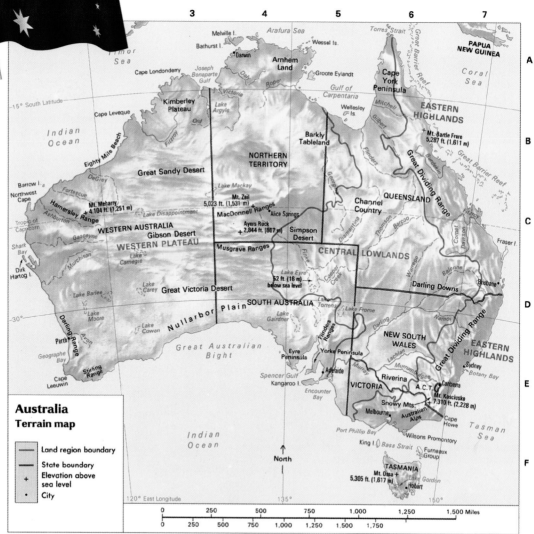

Australia
Terrain map

- Land region boundary
- State boundary
- + Elevation above sea level
- • City

Australia covers about 5 per cent of the earth's land area. Because of its great size, Australia is sometimes called an "island continent." Many places mentioned in this book are shown on the map.

A film poster advertises a *biograph* (motion picture) about the adventures of the bushranger Ned Kelly.

Most notorious outlaw

Ned Kelly (1855-1880) was Australia's most notorious bushranger, or outlaw. He was born at Beveridge in Victoria. Ned Kelly stole horses and cattle, raided banks, and fought gun battles with police, yet to many poor people he seemed a hero. No one took the huge reward offered by the government for his capture.

Kelly, his brother Dan, and two other gang-members hid out in the bush. They made iron helmets and suits of armor for protection. In 1880 they took over the small town of Glenrowan in New South Wales. After an 11-hour siege and shoot-out, three of the gang were killed and Ned Kelly was shot in the legs as he advanced on the police in his iron armor. He was tried, found guilty, and hanged at Melbourne on Nov. 11, 1880.

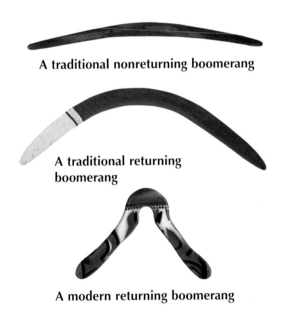

A traditional nonreturning boomerang

A traditional returning boomerang

A modern returning boomerang

Ready, steady, hold on! Camel racing can be tricky, as this rider found out at a sports festival held near Port Hedland in Western Australia.

Will it return?

The boomerang was used in throwing competitions and as a weapon by the Aborigines. Returning boomerangs were made of pieces of thin wood shaped by heating so that one end was twisted upward and the other downward. When thrown correctly, the boomerang flies horizontally at first, then curves upward and returns in a wide circle to the thrower. Nonreturning boomerangs were thrown at kangaroos and other animals pursued by hunters.

Danger: bushfire!

Bushfires (forest, grass, and scrub fires) threaten lives and property in Australia each year. Lightning causes some of these fires, but people are responsible for most of them. February 16, 1983, is remembered as the date of Australia's worst bushfires. On this day, known as Ash Wednesday, 71 people died – 45 in Victoria and 26 in South Australia.

Bushfire brigades fight many blazes each summer, especially in country areas.

TRIGGERED BY FIRE

Banksia is the name of about 70 kinds of plants – from small trees to bushy shrubs – that grow in Australia and New Guinea. Their nutlike seed pods often remain closed for years, until triggered to open by the heat of bushfires.

Banksias are named after the English naturalist Sir Joseph Banks (1743-1820). He financed and led the team of scientists on board Captain James Cook's ship *Endeavour*, which anchored in Botany Bay in 1770.

The southern plains banksia has a cylindrical flower head.

The parma wallaby is a small, rare relative of the kangaroo.

Lost and found

From the 1930's to the 1960's, people thought the parma wallaby was extinct. Then a colony of these generally solitary, nocturnal animals was discovered on a small island off New Zealand, where parma wallabies had been introduced in the 1800's. Another colony was soon discovered in the parma wallaby's native habitat, the eucalyptus forests of northeastern New South Wales.

SEARCHING THE UNIVERSE

Australian science has given us new insights into the universe. The town of Parkes in New South Wales is the site of the Australian National Radio Astronomy Observatory. Its 210-foot (64-meter) radio telescope is one of the world's most accurate astronomical instruments. Opened in 1961, it has pinpointed distant starlike objects called *quasars*.

Aussi-speak

Aussie is used to mean *Australia* or *an Australian*. A Briton is a *Pommy*. You may hear *Tassie* for *Tasmania* and *mozzie* for *mosquito*. Chewing gum is *chewie*, while a *sickie* is a day off school or work for real or pretended illness. A person who is *scungy* is dirty or untidy. Once-popular terms such as *bonzer* for *good*, and *cobber,* meaning *a friend,* are not heard so often nowadays.

A yachting first

In 1983, *Australia II* became the first non-American yacht to win the America's Cup in the 25 challenges from 1870. *Australia II* won the cup at Newport in the United States, beating the U.S. yacht *Liberty* by four races to three.

Anzac Day

Anzac Day is a public holiday in Australia and New Zealand on April 25. The day commemorates the sacrifices made by Australian, New Zealand, and other Allied forces in war. Anzac, the Australian and New Zealand Army Corps, was a combined force of Australian and New Zealand volunteer soldiers formed in Egypt during World War I (1914-1918). Anzac troops gained a reputation for bravery and skill fighting against Turkish forces on the Gallipoli Peninsula from April 1915 to January 1916. In this battle, 7,818 Australian soldiers were killed or died of wounds, and 19,441 men were wounded.

School by radio

The first school of the air was tried experimentally at Alice Springs in 1949, and regular radio-teaching began in 1951. Pupils study at home and talk with teachers by radio.

Schools of the air help children in remote areas to study without attending school.

Australian Olympians

Australia is one of only three nations that have taken part in every Olympic Games since the modern Games began in 1896. The others are Britain and Greece. An Australian competitor in the 1896 Olympics, Edwin Flack, won gold medals in the 800-meter and 1,500-meter races.

The run machine

Cricketer Don Bradman had an amazing run-scoring record. From 1927 to 1949, he scored 28,067 runs, including 117 centuries (scores of more than 100). His career batting average was 95.14, and he played in 52 tests, scoring 6,996 runs at an average of 99.94!

Tasmania's tiger

The Tasmanian tiger, also called the *Tasmanian wolf* or *thylacine*, was a wolflike marsupial predator. Once common in Australia, it lived only on Tasmania when Europeans first came to the continent in the 1700's. The animal was hunted because farmers thought it killed sheep and poultry. Most scientists believe the Tasmanian tiger is now extinct.

Don Bradman scores more runs.

The last Tasmanian tiger? A photograph taken in 1933 shows the last known thylacine in captivity.

Gippsland giants!

The extraordinary Gippsland giant earthworm grows up to 13 feet (4 meters) long. These worms live in burrows near rivers in the Gippsland area of Victoria. The worms slip through their burrows at great speed, and people can hear the distinct gurgling sound they make. The noise is caused as the worms slip through a fluid released from their bodies to lubricate their burrows.

My worm's bigger than your worm. Gippsland's giants are great for worm-lovers!

The Royal Flying Doctor Service

Australia's famous medical service was founded in 1928 by John Flynn and Alfred Traeger, who realized that radio and aircraft could bring medical help to isolated families. Someone in the outback needing medical help can call the nearest radio base to speak to a doctor or arrange for a plane to pick up the patient.

Australia's oldest house

John and Elizabeth Macarthur began the export of wool to England. Their home, Elizabeth Farm, is the oldest house in Australia. The Macarthurs built the house in 1793 on land near Parramatta in New South Wales, and it remained in the family until 1881. The original house had four main rooms, a kitchen, and servants' quarters. Although rooms have been added, the original walls and ceilings are still part of the house.

The Flying Doctor Service brings medical supplies and medical help to people in the Australian outback.

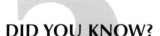

DID YOU KNOW?

There are many Aboriginal place names in Australia. For example:

Kalgoorlie means "three tracks"

Murrumbidgee means "big water"

Parramatta probably means "head of the river"

Wagga Wagga means "many crows"

Canberra means "a meeting place."

From 44 to more than 167 million! The First Fleet brought 44 sheep to Australia in 1788. The country now has more than 167 million – roughly nine sheep for every person.

Glossary

Aborigines First people to live in Australia, originally from Southeast Asia.

aqueduct Channel or pipe built to carry water.

artesian Well in which underground water is pushed by pressure from below up to the surface through a borehole drilled into the earth.

ballad A poem or song that tells a story.

bicentennial Celebration of 200 years.

cargo Goods carried by ship, aircraft or truck.

carnival Festival at which people dance or go in procession through the streets.

canopy Open-sided cover fixed over something to give shelter.

consumer goods Anything that is bought for use by people.

convict A prisoner found guilty (convicted) of a crime.

coral Rock made by small animals in warm seas. A chain of coral makes a reef. A coral cay is a small island.

crossbreds Animals produced from two different breeds.

crude oil Oil in its natural state.

cygnet A young swan.

deformities Things twisted out of shape.

drovers People who drive sheep or cattle.

erode Gradually wear away.

exotic Showy, strange, rich-looking, or foreign.

exporter Person who sends goods to another country to be sold.

extinct Died out, no longer exists.

fangs Long, pointed teeth.

federation Being joined in a group, especially areas of a country or groups of countries.

gold rush A rush of people to a new goldfield.

grand slam The world's four major tennis championships – U.S., French, Australian, and British (Wimbledon).

hydroelectric To do with producing electricity from the power of running water.

immigrants People who come into a country to live.

invertebrates Animals without backbones.

irrigate To carry water to crops through pipes or canals.

isolated Alone, set apart.

mammals Animals whose young live on their mother's milk.

marine park Area reserved for sea animals and plants.

marsupials Mammals whose young are poorly developed and live in their mother's pouch.

metropolitan Belonging to a city.

mineral Hard substance dug out of the earth.

opal A gemstone.

opossum A small, furry marsupial.

organ transplant Operation in which a diseased part of the body is replaced by a healthy part from another person.

Oriental Of the east, especially China and Japan.

permanent Something that lasts for a very long time, or forever.

pest An insect or other animal that damages plants.

pioneer One of the people doing something for the first time.

population All the people who live in a country or area.

prehensile Able to grasp things.

primitive Something at an early stage of development.

regatta Festival of boat or yacht races.

reptile A cold-blooded animal that lays eggs, such as a lizard.

reservoir Lake made to store water for use in cities and towns.

scavengers Animals which pick things clean.

service industries Companies that supply a service rather than make goods.

skin grafting Patching new skin to grow over a wound.

song man Aboriginal singer/storyteller.

Southern Hemisphere Southern half of the world.

species A group of living things with similar characteristics. Animals of the same species can breed with one another.

squatters People who settle on land they want to own.

suburbs Area of houses on the edge of a city or town.

taxidermist Person who prepares, stuffs, and mounts the skin of dead animals.

termite Insect like an ant.

territories Lands that belong to a country.

tropical Anything to do with the area of the earth near the equator, where it is hot all year round.

venom Poison.

virus Tiny germ that causes disease.

volunteers People who offer to do or give something.

Index A page number in **bold** type indicates a picture

Index

Picture acknowledgments
Cover: WORLD BOOK illustration by Arthur Singer; © George Holton, Photo Researchers; © Robert Frerck; Reproduced by courtesy of the artist, George Milpurrurr and the Aboriginal Artist Agency Ltd. (© Robert Frerck); © Peter Simons.

Back Cover: WORLD BOOK illustration by John Charles Pitcher; © Image Bank; © Chuck Nicklin; Press Photo Association; © Eric Worrell, Photographic Library of Australia.

3 Fritz Prenzel (echidna); Ray Kennedy/ *The Age*. Reproduced by permission. 4 WORLD BOOK map; Sydney Opera House. 5 South Australia Tourist Board; Fritz Prenzel. 6 Douglass Baglin; Photographic Library of Australia. 7 Tony Stone Photolibrary, London; Photographic Library of Australia. 8 Photographic Library of Australia. 9 G. R. Roberts (left); © Robert Frerck (right); Photographic Library of Australia (bottom). 10 © Michael Fogden, Earth Scenes; Photographic Library of Australia. 11 Photographic Library of Australia. 12 © Odyssey Productions; J. Allan Cash Photolibrary. 13 Douglass Baglin; Photographic Library of Australia. 14 WORLD BOOK map; photo © Carl Roessler. 15 Photographic Library of Australia; Chuck Nicklin. 17 Earth Scenes; Eric Crichton, Bruce Coleman (right and bottom right). 19 photo L. C. Marigo, Bruce Coleman. 20 Photographic Library of Australia; Warren Garst, Tom Stack & Associates. 21 Photographic Library of Australia; Bruce Coleman. 22 D. B. Croft; Photography Pty Ltd. 23 Bill N. Kleeman, Tom Stack & Associates (top); Warren Garst, Atoz Images (left); Eric Worrell, Photographic Library of Australia (right). 24 © C. Andrew Henley/ N.P.I.A.W. from Nature Focus (top); Robin Smith, Photographic Library of Australia. 25 L & O Schick/Nature Focus (The Australian Museum) (right); Fritz Prenzel; Hans and Judy Beste, Tom Stack & Associates (bottom). 26 © Bill Bachman; Photographic Library of Australia. 27 © Philip Quirk, Wildlight; J. Allan Cash Photolibrary 28 Scene from a production by the Lyric Opera of Chicago with Regina Resnik (left), Joan Sutherland (second from right), and Spiro Malas (WORLD BOOK photo); United Press International (top); Australian High Commission, London. 29 Ray Kennedy/*The Age*. Reproduced by permission. 30 Australian Overseas Information Service, London. 31 Richard Desgrand; Photographic Library of Australia. 32 Tony Stone Photolibrary, London (bottom). 33 Don Stephens. 34 Nick Servian, Robert Harding Picture Library. 35 © Robert Frerck.; © Richard Desgrand.. 36 Fritz Prenzel. 37 Tony Stone Photolibrary, London; Richard Desgrand (left); Mitchell Library (bottom). 38 David Moore, Black Star. 39 Grant Heilman. 40 David Moore, Black Star. 41 Jeff Carter (top); © James L. Stanfield, National Geographic Society. 42 G. R. Roberts (top); Tourism South Australia. 43 Photographic Library of Australia. 44 Robert Harding Picture Library. 45 BHP; ESSO. 46 © Robert Frerck; John Start, Robert Harding Picture Library. 47 © Nick Rains, Australian Picture Library; Photographic Library of Australia. 48 © Peter Simons; J. Allan Cash Photolibrary. 49 Douglass Baglin; Photographic Library of Australia. 50 Victorian Football League; National Museum, Victoria; David Moore, Black Star (bottom). 51 Photographic Library of Australia. 52 J. Allan Cash Photolibrary; Image Bank. 53 Greg Bowman; © Robert Frerck. 54 Reproduced by courtesy of the artist, George Milpurrurr, and of the Aboriginal Art Agency Ltd. (© Robert Frerck); Richard Desgrand. 55 The Mitchell Library (top); Australian War Memorial; Tate Gallery, London/Art Resource (bottom). 56 WORLD BOOK map. 57 National Film and Sound Archive, Australia; (boomerangs) Benjamin Ruhe Collection (WORLD BOOK photo by Vince Finnigan & Assoc.); Benjamin Ruhe Collection (WORLD BOOK photo by Vince Finnigan & Assoc.); WORLD BOOK illustration by Ted Bailey; © Robert Frerck. 58 Jan Taylor/Bruce Coleman; G. R. Roberts (wallaby); Photographic Library of Australia (bushfire). 59 ZEFA; © Bill Bachman. 60 Press Association (top); David Fleay; Australian Museum/Nature Focus (worms). 61 Photographic Library of Australia.

Illustrations
By WORLD BOOK artists including Tom Dolan, Walter Linsenmaier, Harry McNaught, Oxford Illustrators Ltd., John Rignall/Linden Artists, and James Teason.